The water's deep,
The sharks are thin,
The current's strong
So COME ON IN!

First published 1987 by Walker Books Ltd
87 Vauxhall Walk, London SE11 5HJ

This edition published 2003

This book has been typeset in Plantin

Printed in Great Britain
by St Edmundsbury Press, Bury St Edmunds

British Library Cataloguing in Publication Data:
a catalogue record for this book is
available from the British Library

ISBN 0-7445-9088-4

www.walkerbooks.co.uk

THERE'S AN AWFUL LOT OF WEIRDOS IN OUR NEIGHBOURHOOD

A Book of Rather Silly Poems and Pictures

Colin McNaughton

Foreword by the Ahlbergs

WALKER BOOKS
AND SUBSIDIARIES
LONDON • BOSTON • SYDNEY

For Sebastian

FOREWORD
by the Ahlbergs

Dear Boys and Girls (and mums and dads
and aunties and uncles and grandmas and long
lost cousins), here is a book of poems and pictures
by our good friend, Colin McNaughton.
We love Colin. He's funny, kind,
talented – and he pays well!

Colin, by the way, comes of a large family.
He and his eight brothers are extremely close.
So please buy this book. You won't regret it.
Whereas, if you *don't* buy it, and the
McNaughton Brothers get to hear –
you *will* regret it.

CROCODILE FEARS

"I found this in the stream," said Mabel.
"I thought it might do for the nature table!"

IF YOU FIND THAT YOUR DINOSAUR'S LAZY AND SLOW

If you find that your dinosaur's
Lazy and slow,
Won't do what he's told,
Lost his "get up and go",
Then take my advice,
I won't charge you a cent,
Just follow these rules,
It's money well spent.

You must really get cross
And show him who's boss.
Give him a smack
And shout "GET MOVIN' MAC!"
Then punch his nose
And step on his toes.
If he starts to complain
That you're causing him pain,
Twist his arm up his back
Till his bones almost crack
And say:
"Now will you do what you're told?"

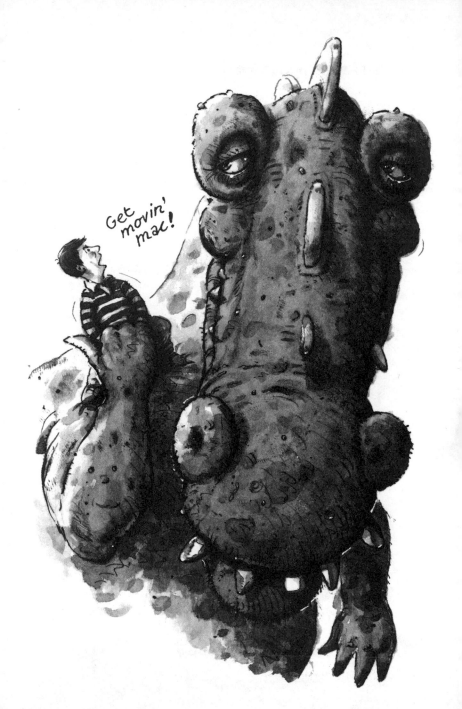

11

I HAVE AN OASIS

I have an oasis,
It's up in the clouds
Away from the rush
And the roar of the crowds,
Away from the pushing
And pulling and pain,
Away from the sadness
And anger and strain,
Away from the envy
And cheating and greed,
Away from the pressure –
What more could I need?
I grow my geraniums
And lettuce that's curled,
In my little garden
On top of the world.

POOR LITTLE ARABELLA

Poor little Arabella,
Why didn't someone tell her
Not to use her umbrella
When the north wind blows?

SICK OF BEING PUSHED AROUND?

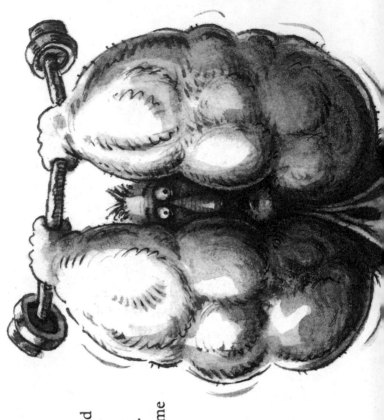

Sick of being
Pushed around,
I sent away
For a course I'd found
In a Batman comic;
Only cost one pound.
It promised to make me
Musclebound.
I must say I quite
Liked the sound
Of a powerful body
That would astound!
They sent part one,
My arms look great!

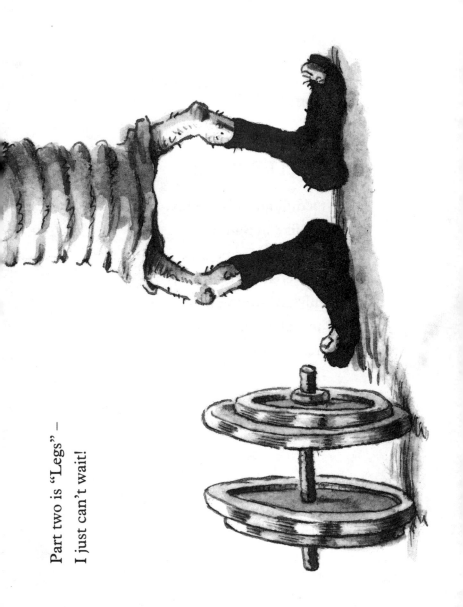

Part two is "Legs" –
I just can't wait!

WINTER POEM

It's dull and it's cloudy,
Not like in Saudi
Arabia or Katmandu.
It's wet and it's windy,
Unlike Rawalpindi,
I'm sick of this weather –
Aren't you?

MONDAY'S CHILD IS RED AND SPOTTY

Monday's child is red and spotty,
Tuesday's child won't use the potty.
Wednesday's child won't go to bed,
Thursday's child will not be fed.
Friday's child breaks all his toys,
Saturday's child makes an awful noise.
And the child that's born on the seventh day
Is a pain in the neck like the rest, OK!

I HAD A LITTLE NUT TREE

I had a little nut tree,
Nothing would it grow,
So I dug it up and burned it…
and bought an apple tree instead.

A LOAD OF OLD TRIPE

My cousin Davey
Eats anything with gravy:
Chocolate cake, ice-cream or peas!
But I prefer tripe
When it's lukewarm and ripe
And it slobbers all over your knees!

Mon Oncle Pierre
Is a gourmand, I swear.
He eats things like frogs' legs and eels!
But I prefer tripe
When it's lukewarm and ripe
Which I gobble before it congeals!

My nephew Jake
Is as thin as a rake,
His diet is snails in their shells!
But I prefer tripe
When it's lukewarm and ripe –
Slightly yellowing, runny and smells!

Grandfather Sid
Would eat his boiled squid
Till it squirted out both of his ears!
But I prefer tripe
When it's lukewarm and ripe
Washed down with a couple of beers!

P.T.O. ➔

My mum, rest her soul,
Could swallow a bowl
Of giblets that we thought were off!
But I prefer tripe
When it's lukewarm and ripe
(Best eaten alone at a trough!)

My big brother Todd
I think of as odd:
Hamburgers and pizzas he loves!
While I prefer tripe
When it's lukewarm and ripe
Which I eat wearing thick rubber gloves.

Grandmother Dinah,
Who's travelled in China,
Eats birds' eggs a thousand years old!
But I prefer tripe
When it's lukewarm and ripe,
And green round the edges with mould.

So as you can see,
There's but one dish for me –
It's tripe in its natural state.
If you ask me my taste,
Then your time I won't waste –
It's a load of old tripe on a plate!

JUST CALL ME "RAT"!

My brother's name is Edward,
My sister's name is Pat.
  My mum and dad
  Are Rose and Brad.
And me? Just call me "Rat"!

DON'T PUT SUGAR IN MY TEA, MUM

Don't put sugar in my tea, Mum.
Don't put sugar in my tea.
I'm already fat,
So that's enough of that.
Don't put sugar in my tea.

I'M MUCH BETTER THAN YOU

My dad's bigger than your dad,
Got more money too.
My house is posher than your house –
I'm much better than you.

My mum's prettier than your mum,
Our car is faster too.
We have a house in the country –
I'm much better than you.

My toys cost more than your toys,
My clothes are trendier too.
My school costs more than your school –
I'm much better than you.

We have a maid and a nanny,
We have a gardener too.
I'm driven to school by our chauffeur –
I'm much better than you.

Our summers we spend in Tahiti,
In winter we ski in Peru.
My cousin Di's married royalty –
I'm much better than…

At this point the poem comes to a terrible end when an armed and extremely dangerous grizzly bear, *Ursus horribilis*, who is on the run from the maximum security wing of London Zoo and who has not eaten for three days, leaps from behind a tree and swallows up the boy without so much as a "How do you do?"

– Sad, eh?

I PLANTED SOME SEEDS

I planted some seeds
In my garden today.
They haven't come up yet,
I hope they're okay.

Should I dig them all up,
Take them back to the shop?
Ask for my money back,
Say they're a flop?

Perhaps they were faulty,
Perhaps they were duff,
Maybe they haven't
Been watered enough.

I planted some seeds
In my garden today.
They haven't come up yet,
I hope they're okay.

THE WERST POME
WOT I EVER RITTED

Roses are read,
Vilets are bloo.
Do yoo luv me?
Cos I luv her.

SO WHAT!

If I still have a dummy, so what!
If I cuddle my mummy, so what!
I'll stop when I'm ready,
And as for my teddy,
If he helps me to sleep, then SO WHAT!

PERMIT HOLDERS ONLY

Daddy had an argument
   on Friday night,
With a man from outer space.
Daddy said, "I don't care
   where you're from,
You're in my parking place!"

SHORT SHARP SHOCK

If your children are ever unruly,
(Of course this might never happen),
Just tell them to kindly behave themselves,
Then reach over quickly and slap 'em!

LEMMY WAS A DIVER

Lemmy was a diver,
A deep-sea diver.
Lemmy was a diver,
Five years old.

Lemmy found a treasure chest,
A chock-full treasure chest.
Lemmy found a treasure chest,
Stuffed with gold!

But Lemmy had a rival, oh,
A twenty-two ton rival, oh.
Yes, Lemmy had a rival, oh,
A great white whale.

He took a classic pose, sir,
And bopped him on the nose, sir.
Cos that's how you dispose, sir,
Of twenty-two ton whales.

Now Lemmy is a rich boy,
A fabulously rich boy.
He's lost the diving itch, boy.
But now instead –

Lemmy is a pilot,
A top-notch pilot.
Lemmy is a pilot,
Six years old.

I THOUGHT I'D TAKE MY RAT
TO SCHOOL

I thought I'd take my rat to school
To show my nice new teacher.
"Aaaeeeiiiiiiieeaa!" she said.
"Get out, you horrid creature!"

FINGERS

1, 2, 3, 4, 5, 6, 7, 8, 9, 10.
And then...
10, 9, 8, 7, 6, 5, 4, 3, 2, 1.
All gone!

THERE'S AN AWFUL LOT OF WEIRDOS IN OUR NEIGHBOURHOOD

There's an awful lot of weirdos
   In our neighbourhood!
Yes, there's an awful lot of weirdos
   In our neighbourhood!

I know this physical wreck,
   Who has a bolt through his neck!
There's an awful lot of weirdos
   In our neighbourhood.

And in an upstairs room,
   An old lady rides a broom!
There's an awful lot of weirdos
   In our neighbourhood.

A man lives on the square,
   When he's in he isn't there!
There's an awful lot of weirdos
   In our neighbourhood.

And that woman down the block,
   Whose snaky hair's a shock!
There's an awful lot of weirdos
   In our neighbourhood.

We've a strange old feller,
   With horns, down in the cellar!
There's an awful lot of weirdos
   In our neighbourhood.

There's a guy who's green and scaly,
   Has webbed feet and sells fish daily!
There's an awful lot of weirdos
   In our neighbourhood.

And someone near the dairy,
   When the moon is out gets hairy!
There's an awful lot of weirdos
   In our neighbourhood.

Think I'll leave this miscellanea,
   And return to Transylvania,
'cause there's an awful lot of weirdos
   In our neighbourhood!

I'm off!

I HAVE NEVER BEEN SO HAPPY

I have never been so happy
   Since my dear old mom and pappy
Packed the car and left real snappy,
   Said they'd had enough.

I can eat just what I feel like,
   Make up any kind of meal, like
Mars bars, chips and jellied eels, like
   Mommy never made.

To nursery school I gave up going,
   They teach you nothing that's worth knowing,
And anyway there's movies showing
   In the afternoons.

And bedtime, well, it's up to me now,
Midnight, two or half past three now.
Sometimes I'll just watch TV now
All night long.

So if you're listening, mom and pappy,
As you can see I'm really happy,
But could you come and change my nappy,
Mommy, Pappy, please!

DUNCE

I always try my hardest,
I always do my best.
It's just that I don't seem to be
As clever as the rest.

THE ELIBIRD

Who's ever heard of the Elibird?
Sounds absurd, an Elibird.
One third's bird, two third's furred –
The body of an elephant, take my word.

51

I WAS BRAVE AND I WAS BOLD

When I played football for my team
I was the best they'd ever seen.

See me dribble, see me pass.
Watch me move across the grass.
I was fast and I was cunning,
I was brilliant at running.
I would score ten goals a game,
Every match would be the same.
Shots from near and shots from far.
Headers, backheels – what a star!
Fans would shout out for their hero
When I'd made it fifteen-zero!

I was brave and I was bold,
And I was only eight years old.

ON REFLECTION

When I look in the mirror
What do I see...?

NOSY PORKER

How do you do?
How do you don't?
How do you will?
How do you won't?
How's your father?
How's your mother?
How's your sister?
How's your brother?
How's your dog?
How's your cat?
How's your mouse?
How's your rat?
How's your walls?
How's your floors?
How's your roofs?
How's your doors?
How's your table?
How's your chairs?
How's your apples?
How's your pears?
How's your cold?
How's your cough?
How's the time?
Must be off!

MUGSY O'SHEA

Is this the end for Mugsy?
  It sure brings a tear to your eye.
Is this the end for Mugsy O'Shea?
  The poor kid is too young to die!

Is this the end for Mugsy?
  Cut down in his prime.
Is this the end for Mugsy O'Shea,
  The end of his life of crime?

Is this the end for Mugsy?
  I think when it comes to the crunch,
This isn't the end for Mugsy O'Shea –
  He'll recover in time for his lunch!

HOW MANY STARS?

When I was a boy
I would ask my dad:
"How many stars are there hanging in the sky?"
"More than enough, son,
More than I could say.
Enough to keep you counting
Till your dying day."

When I was a boy
I would ask my dad:
"How many fishes are there swimming in the sea?"
"More than enough, son,
More than I could say.
Enough to keep you counting
Till your dying day."

When I was a boy
I would ask my dad:
"How many creepy-crawlies are there in the world?"
"More than enough, son.
More than I could say.
Enough to keep you counting
Till your dying day."

It seemed like there wasn't anything
my dad didn't know.

MY CAT

My cat gives me serious cause for concern.
I've tried, but I do not know which way to turn.
It's not just the suit or the paisley cravat
Or the pink patent boots; I can handle all that.
But now he's developed a worrying trait:
He's mugging my guests as they come through the gate!

He's stealing their pants and their shirts and their ties,
Although he denies it and says it's all lies.
Should I call the police or the vet or the zoos?
Should I offer to buy him his clothing and shoes?
I've tried, but I do not know which way to turn –
My cat gives me serious cause for concern.

WHAT DO YOU SAY, SIR?

What do you say, Sir?
You've got to admit,
For twenty-five pence,
It's a very good fit!

YOU'D BETTER BEWARE
(A Reptile Rap)

You'd better beware, if you come round here,
To watch your step, to steer well clear
Of my front gate, it's a dangerous place
Because you might come face to face
With my new pet who's big and mean,
The ugliest brute you've ever seen.

Crooks and robbers don't come near,
They creep right past, they shake with fear.
They'd rather spend a year in gaol
Than risk one tickle from his fingernail.
Claws like razors, teeth like knives,
They'd better get lost, better run for their lives.

So if you're broke or out of work,
Get pushed around and called a jerk,
And if you're sad or if you're blue,
Take my advice, this is what you do:
Go down to the monster store
And get yourself a dinosaur.

Beat that drum, bang that gong,
Six metres high by sixteen long,
Come on all join in the chorus:
My new pet's a Tyrannosaurus!

THE HUMAN SIREN

Tim, Tim, the human siren,
LOUDEST boy in town.
Tim, Tim, the human siren,
Never lets you down.

Tim, Tim, the human siren,
When he's not at play,
We rent him to the fire brigade
At fifteen pounds a day.

TRACY VENABLES

Tracy Venables thinks she's great,
Swinging on her garden gate.
She's the girl I love to hate –
"Show-off" Tracy Venables.

She's so fat she makes me sick,
Eating ice-cream, lick, lick, lick.
I know where I'd like to kick
"Stink-pot" Tracy Venables.

Now she's shouting 'cross the street,
What's she want, the dirty cheat?
Would I like some? Oh, how sweet
Of my friend Tracy Venables.

I AM A JOLLY GIANT

I am a jolly giant,
I have no cares or woes,
If you don't give me all your cash,
I'll punch you in the nose.

HIDE-AND-SEEK

wonoothreefourfisisernayniten-readyornothereIcome

THE GIANTS ARE HAVING A PARTY

The giants who live next to us
Don't usually cause any fuss,
Except once a year,
When they let down their hair,
And party the night away thus:

Wee-ha! Yahoo! Bonk! Yoo-hoo!
Hee-hoo! Wing-ding! Conk! Boo-hoo!
Wah-hoo! Tee-hee! Zonk! Coo-hoo!
Hoo-hee! Yah-boo! Gonk! Poo-poo!

Thump, thumpa, thumpeta thump!
Barumpeta dumpeta dump!
Barumpeta-thump!
Barumpeta-whump!
Barumpeta-thumpeta bump!

I say, boop bee doo,
Hoop-dap-dee-dah-boogle-ooh!
Chickety-bak-dik,
Dickety-bak-chick!
Flickety-dickety-chickety-bak,
Oop-oop-pee-do!

Thud, thud, wahoo, thud!
Yeeha, wahoo, thud!
Dump, dump, flumpity flump!
Crumpity! Crumpity! Thump!

A reep dap-a-cooney.
Riddle daddle mooney.
A-bobble-wobble looney,
Diddly-bang-po!

Do wop a do wop a do wop a do.
Do wop a rang dong a ging gang goo.
Ooh wap a do wap a do wap a do.
Shoo wop a loo mop a bing bang boo!

Yee-ha whoops bang!
Yee-ha whoops bang!
A-thumpa-dumpa-whumpa!
Crack, bump, squelch!
Bang whoops ye-ha
Bang whoops yee-ha
A whumpa dumpa thumpa,
Gobble, slurp, belch!

A POEM TO SEND TO YOUR WORST ENEMY

Ugly Mug,
Fat Belly!
Slimy Slug,
Smelly Welly!

Silly Nit,
What a Pain!
Armpit,
Bird Brain!

Dum Dum,
Ghosty Ghool!
Big Bum,
Stupid Fool!

Pig Face,
Dopey Twit!
Nut Case,
You're IT!

TEEF! TEEF!

Teef! Teef!
I've loshed my teef!
Hash anyone sheen my teef?
You won't be able to help, I shuppose;
But shombody shtole them from
Under my nose!
Hash anyone sheen my teef?

HAIR PIECE

You may have noticed
The grizzly bear
Is completely, totally
Covered with hair.

And slithering through
The grass, you'll see,
The snake's as bald
As a processed pea.

But I'm in between
Although not 'cos I'm careless:
There's hair on my head,
While the rest of me's hairless.
(well, almost)

A processed pea
Is easily
The greenest thing
You'll ever see.

FISHY TALE

My friend Brian says
that all the people who live in Finland
have fins because they eat so much fish.
My dad says it's not true
but I think it might be.

ABSURD BIRD WORDS

I made the mistake
Of teaching some birds
A collection of horribly
Difficult words.

Not one word of thanks
Have I heard from their beaks.
They just sit there all day,
Quoting Latins and Greeks.

85

A YBALLUL

Hazy Maisy
Upsy-daisy
Out of bed and
Don't be lazy.

Wakey, wakey,
New day yawning,
Rise and shine and
Say "good morning".

I DON'T WANT TO GO INTO SCHOOL

I don't want to go into school today, Mum,
I don't feel like schoolwork today.
Oh, don't make me go into school today, Mum,
Oh, please let me stay home and play.

But you must go to school, my cherub, my lamb.
If you don't it will be a disaster.
How would they manage without you, my sweet,
After all, you are the headmaster!

A FAT LOT OF GOOD

Our vicar is kind,
But eats more than he should.
I suppose we could call him,
"A fat lot of good."

LUCY MARGOLIS

Lucy Margolis,
An only child,
When her parents were cross,
Just looked up and smiled,
Said: "Goo-goo, ga goo-goo,
Ga goo-goo, ga-goo."
And her parents forgave her.
Well, wouldn't you?

I WISH I WAS NORMAL

I wish I was normal
Like everyone else.
I wish I was normal
Like you.
I wish I was normal
Like everyone else.
I wish I had one head,
Not two.

I hate being normal
Like everyone else.
Being normal is not
Any fun!
I hate being normal
Cos everyone knows
That two heads are better
Than one!

MY BEST PAL

There's a boy in our class
Name of Billy McMillan,
And everyone knows
He's a bit of a villain.

My mum doesn't like him,
No more does my dad,
They say he's a hooligan;
This makes me mad.

Okay, so he's scruffy
And hopeless at school,
But that doesn't mean he's
An absolute fool.

He's brilliant at spitting
And juggling with balls,
And no one can beat him
At peeing up walls.

He's my best mate
And I think he's just fine,
You can choose your friends,
And I will choose mine.

CROCODILE'S KIN

The best use for a crocodile skin
Is to keep a crocodile's insides in.

THE INVITATION

Here's my invitation:
Some giants I know
Have asked me to dinner –
I don't think I'll go!

We might have had chicken
Or a nice piece of ham,
Or duck à l'orange
Stuffed with blackberry jam.

It could have been beefsteak
With green beans and chips,
Or roast lamb in cider
With 'sparagus tips.

Suppose it were pork chops
With mustard and cress,
Or thick rabbit stew
And a hot bouillabaisse?

What if it were dumplings
With carrots and mince
Garnished with lemmings,
Each stuffed with a quince?

Or what about pies
Made with pigeons and hares
And partridge and pheasant
And Kodiak bears?

Caviar, octopus,
Squid by the score,
Followed by boiled
Portuguese-Man-o'-War.

Then blackcurrant crumble
And crème caramel,
Lashings of ice-cream
And custard as well.

Cheeses and salads
And jelly and sweets,
Fine wines and coffee
And hundreds more treats!

I may be mistaken,
Distrustful, maybe –
But I think the main course
Was meant to be ME!

SLOW, SLOW, THICK, THICK SNOW

If you want to get from A to B
I'll give you this advice for free:
You'll find that cycling in the snow
Is not the quickest way to go.

FEE-FI-FO-HUM!

Fee-fi-fo-fum!
I smell the pong of an Englishman.
Be he alive or be he dead,
I wish he were somewhere else instead!

PICKING NOSES

When I was young
I picked my nose.
I just said,
"Gimme one of those!"

Now I've gone off
The one I chose;
You wouldn't swap,
I don't suppose?

SNIFF

Caught a cold, sniff.
Feel all funny, sniff.
Eyes are red, sniff.
Nose is runny, sniff.
Can't complain, sniff.
I'm no fool, sniff.
One good thing, sniff.
Week off school…
SNIFF!

I LOVE YOU BECAUSE
(A Monster Duet)

You're fat and lumpy,
Ugly and grumpy,
Hairy, green and grimy.
You're big and smelly,
Sticky-out belly.
Oily, wet and slimy.
And that's why I love you.

CRAZY FRANKIE

Crazy Frankie's round the twist,
Cross him off your party list.
He'd beat your guests up, wreck your house,
Call your dad "a dirty louse"!
Open your presents, stuff his face,
Sick it up all over the place.
Break the windows, kick the cat,
Call your gran "a dirty rat"!
Rip your books and mix your jigsaws,
Laughing hee-haw, hee-haw, hee-haws.
Smash your toys and let your tyres down,
Cut the sleeves off your mum's nightgown.
Cross him off your party list;
Crazy Frankie's round the twist!

NASTY NAT

Nasty Nat,
Total brat.
Back chat,
Yap! Yap!
Yah, boo!
The lot of you.

Smack!

Take that!
Nasty Nat.

THE GARDEN'S FULL OF WITCHES

Mum! The garden's full of witches!
Come quick and see the witches.
    There's a full moon out,
    And they're flying about,
Come on! You'll miss the witches.

Oh Mum! You're missing the witches.
You have never seen so many witches.
    They are casting spells!
    There are horrible smells!
Come on! You'll miss the witches.

Mum, hurry! Come look at the witches.
The shrubbery's bursting with witches.
    They've turned our Joan
    Into a garden gnome.
Come on! You'll miss the witches.

Oh no! You'll miss the witches.
The garden's black with witches.
    Come on! Come on!
    Too late! They've gone.
Oh, you always miss the witches!

A PERFECT FIT

"A perfect fit!"
Said the man in the shop.
"A mite tight at the bottom,
And loose at the top.
We'll just take it in here
And lose a bit there.
We'll shorten the sleeves
And sew up that tear.
We'll move all the buttons
Before you can blink,
Then build up the shoulders –
Now what do you think?

We could put in some pockets
And patch up the knees,
Sponge out the egg stains –
Our aim is to please.
We'll lengthen the trousers
And fix that old zip,
Then take in the waist
And let out the hip.
Now what do you say, Sir,
How does it feel?
Do you want to buy it?
Have we got a deal?"

"No, you do not, Sir!
Because, to begin with,
It's already mine –
It's the suit I came in with!"

AT LONG LAST,
SPRING HAS ARRIVED!

At long last, spring has arrived.
"So there you are!" I said icily.
"About time too!" I said frostily.
"You're late!" I said coldly.

"Cool it," she said mildly.
"I've been under a lot of pressure lately.
Have a daffodil."

"Blooming cheek," I said,
In the heat of the moment.

THE LESSON

"Blether, blather, blah-blah, bosh.
Claptrap, humbug, poppycock, tosh.
Guff, flap-doodle, gas and gabble.
Hocus pocus, gibberish, babble.
Baloney, hooey, jabber, phew,
Stuff and nonsense, drivel, moo.
Rhubarb, rhubarb, rhubarb, banter.
Prattle, waffle, rave and ranter.
Rubbish, piffle, tommy-rot, guff,
Twaddle, bilge, bombast, bluff.

Thank you."

BORER THE EXPLORER

Back in 1920,
In the jungles of Fwadong.
The heat was getting hotter,
And my socks began to pong.

I was eaten by an elephant,
But I didn't really care.
It was cooler in his belly,
I had plenty room in there.

But when he ate a tiger
I felt I must protest.
I couldn't stretch my legs out.
A most unwelcome guest.

So taking out my telephone,
And dialling Timbuctoo,
I asked to speak to Tarzan.
The lady put me through.

"Greetings, Tarzan! King of Apes.
Explorer Borer here.
Could you come and rescue me,
And bring some ginger beer?"

"Me making movie at this time.
Me cannot come right now.
Me be there soon as possible.
My schedule will allow."

It's not that I'm ungrateful,
But Tarzan took his time.
He didn't get me out of there
Till 1959.

A HEART OF GOLD

I'm rich! I'm rich!
I've just been told
That I have got
A heart of gold.

I might sell it,
But I doubt it.
Don't think I could
Live without it.

INDEX